T0401514

Life in Numbers

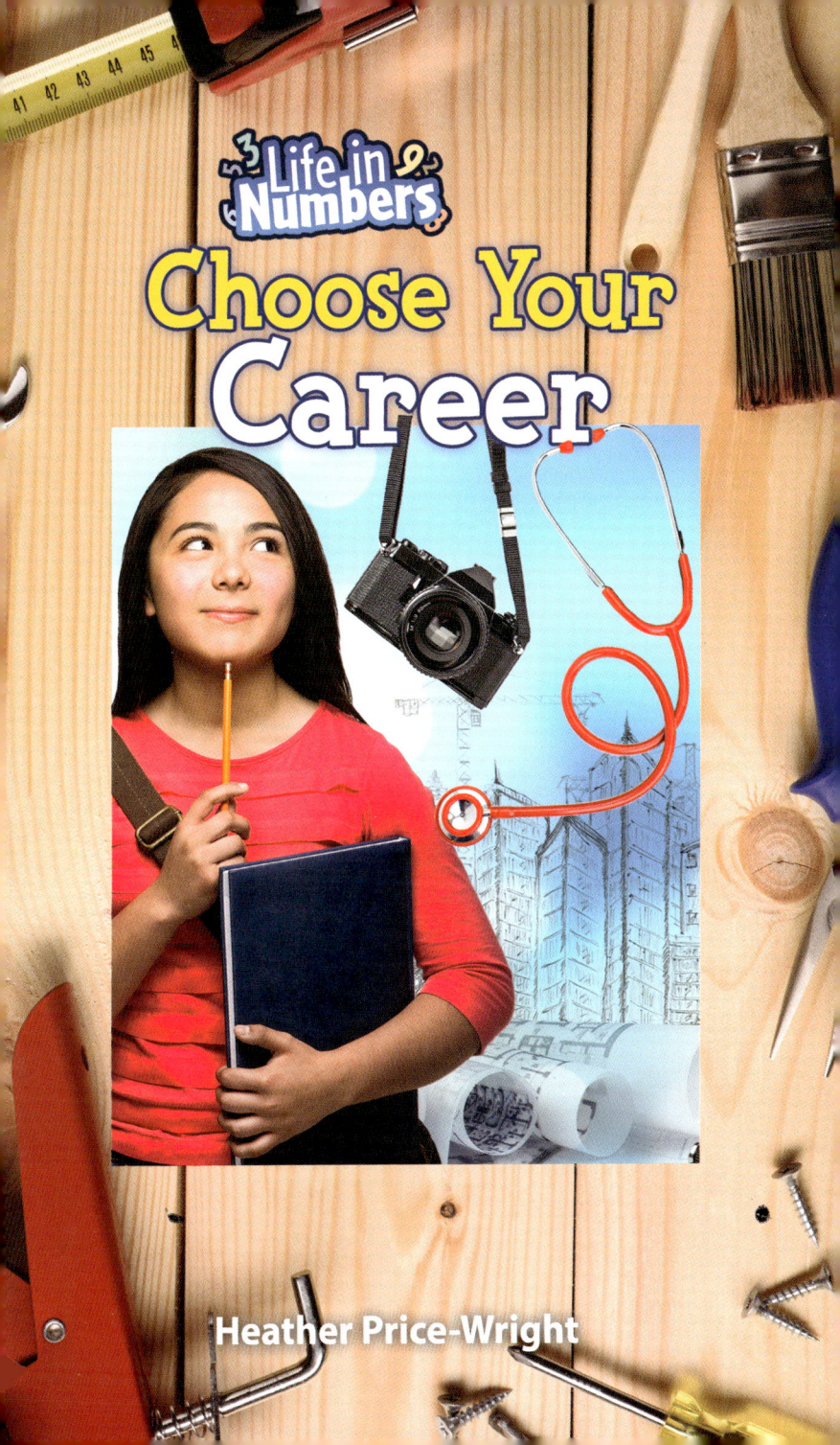

Choose Your Career

Heather Price-Wright

Publishing Credits

Rachelle Cracchiolo, M.S.Ed., *Publisher*
Conni Medina, M.A.Ed., *Managing Editor*
Nika Fabienke, Ed.D., *Series Developer*
June Kikuchi, *Content Director*
Seth Rogers, *Editor*
Michelle Jovin, M.A., *Assistant Editor*
Lee Aucoin, *Senior Graphic Designer*

TIME For Kids and the TIME For Kids logo are registered trademarks of TIME Inc. Used under license.

Image Credits: p.5 Anton_Ivanov/Shutterstock.com; pp.14–15 Agencja Fotograficzna Caro/Alamy Stock Photo; p.16 Bygone Collection/Alamy Stock Photo; pp.18–19 Historical Art Collection (HAC)/Alamy Stock Photo; p.22 Stock Montage/Getty Images; p.38 Entertainment Pictures/Alamy Stock Photo; p.40 Library of Congress [LC-USW33-042784-ZC]; all other images from iStock and/or Shutterstock.

All companies and products mentioned in this book are registered trademarks of their respective owners or developers and are used in this book strictly for editorial purposes; no commercial claim to their use is made by the author or the publisher.

Library of Congress Cataloging-in-Publication Data

Names: Price-Wright, Heather.
Title: Life in numbers : choose your career / Heather Price-Wright.
Description: Huntington Beach, CA : Teacher Created Materials, [2017] | Audience: Grades 4 to 6. | Includes index.
Identifiers: LCCN 2017023522 (print) | LCCN 2017027226 (ebook) | ISBN 9781425853594 (eBook) | ISBN 9781425849856 (pbk.)
Subjects: LCSH: Career development--Juvenile literature.
Classification: LCC HF5381.2 (ebook) | LCC HF5381.2 .P745 2017 (print) | DDC 331.702--dc23
LC record available at https://lccn.loc.gov/2017023522

Teacher Created Materials

5301 Oceanus Drive
Huntington Beach, CA 92649-1030
http://www.tcmpub.com
ISBN 978-1-4258-4985-6
© 2018 Teacher Created Materials, Inc.
Made in China
Nordica.092017.CA21701119

Table of Contents

All About Work 4

All About You 8

Working with Purpose 16

The Numbers Game 20

Off the Beaten Path 30

Make a Plan 38

Glossary 42

Index 44

Check It Out! 46

Try It! 47

About the Author 48

All About Work

Imagine yourself in the future. It is early morning, you have just finished breakfast, and now you are heading out the door. Maybe you are wearing a suit, or maybe you slip into a white doctor's coat and drape a stethoscope around your neck. Perhaps you are in a police uniform, or sporting bright, cheerful colors to appeal to the kindergarten students you teach. Maybe you are wearing jeans and a hoodie. It all depends on your career.

A great deal of effort goes into choosing the right career. The first step is to think about who you are and what you want to do.

Drive Time

Studies show that people with shorter commutes tend to be happier. But longer commutes are now more common in the United States. It takes Americans an average of 26 minutes to travel to work. That means, in total, Americans spend almost 30 billion hours a year getting to and from work. In that time, Americans could build the Great Pyramid of Giza. In fact, they could build it 26 times!

Work Clothes

Some highly successful people suggest wearing the same style of clothes every day. Steve Jobs (the founder of Apple, shown right) and Albert Einstein both thought it was a good idea. That way, you don't use extra brainpower choosing a new outfit each day. Instead, you can use the time to think about ways to improve your work.

Choosing the right career can be **daunting**. There are many career paths from which to choose. But many jobs fit into a few key industries.

Health, finance, technology, manufacturing, and retail are all huge industries in the United States. These words may sound **vague**, but each one has many career paths. For example, a career in finance could mean a job at a bank. It could also mean keeping track of the budget for a charity. The options in these industries are limitless.

Tech Tools

Within health care, one of the biggest **sectors** is health technology. These workers use high-tech tools to help people get and stay healthy. Many people think robots may soon be able to do this job!

Measuring Success

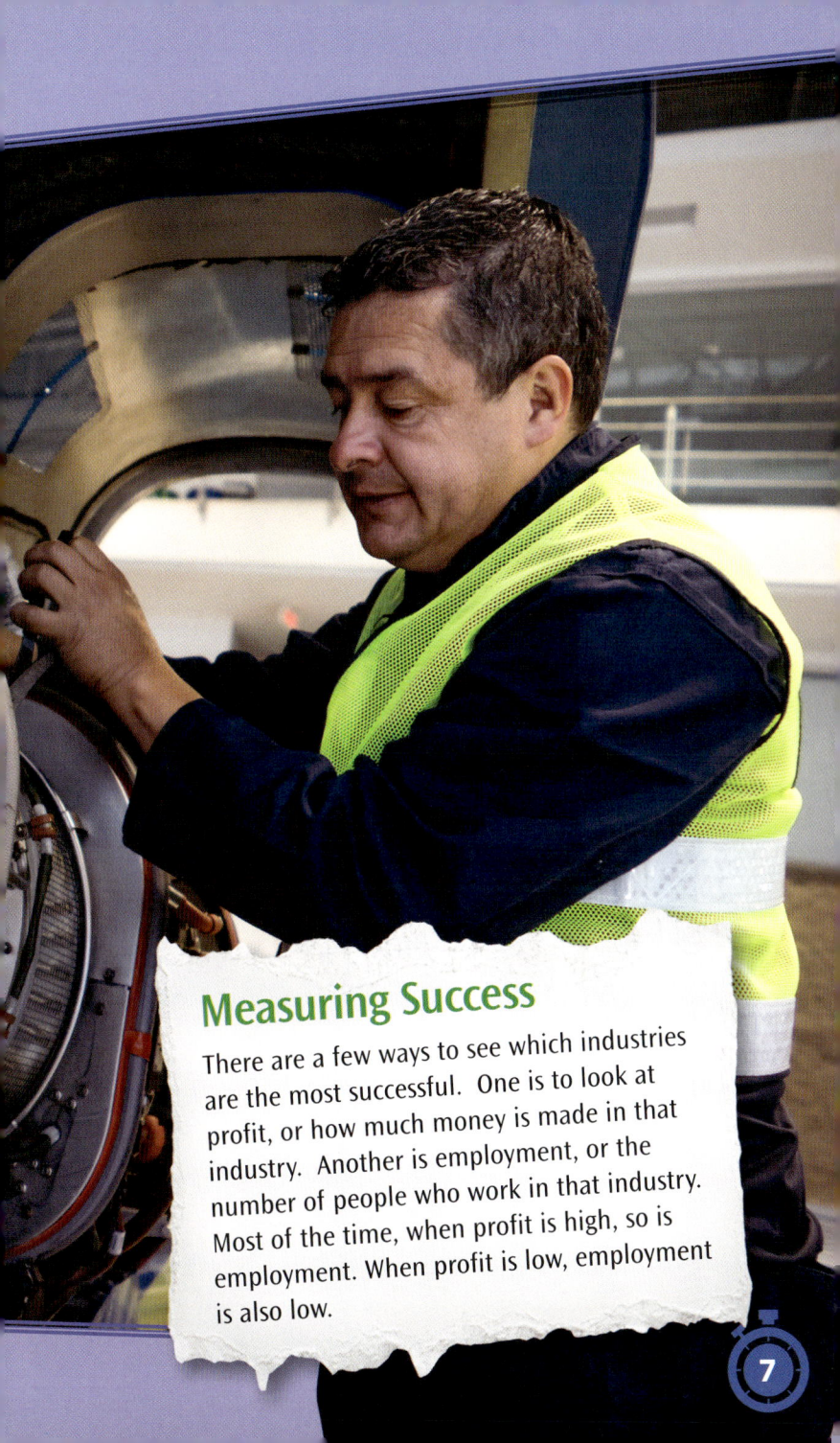

There are a few ways to see which industries are the most successful. One is to look at profit, or how much money is made in that industry. Another is employment, or the number of people who work in that industry. Most of the time, when profit is high, so is employment. When profit is low, employment is also low.

All About You

Young people have plenty of time to figure out what career they want, but it is never too early to start thinking about the future. The earlier people start planning, the clearer their paths will be.

What Do You Like?

Your likes and dislikes matter a great deal when it comes to choosing the right career. Think about your favorite hobbies and your favorite subject in school. Would you rather sit quietly and read, or are you an active person? Do you like spending time alone, in a small group of close friends, or in a big group? The answers to all of these questions can help you narrow your career options.

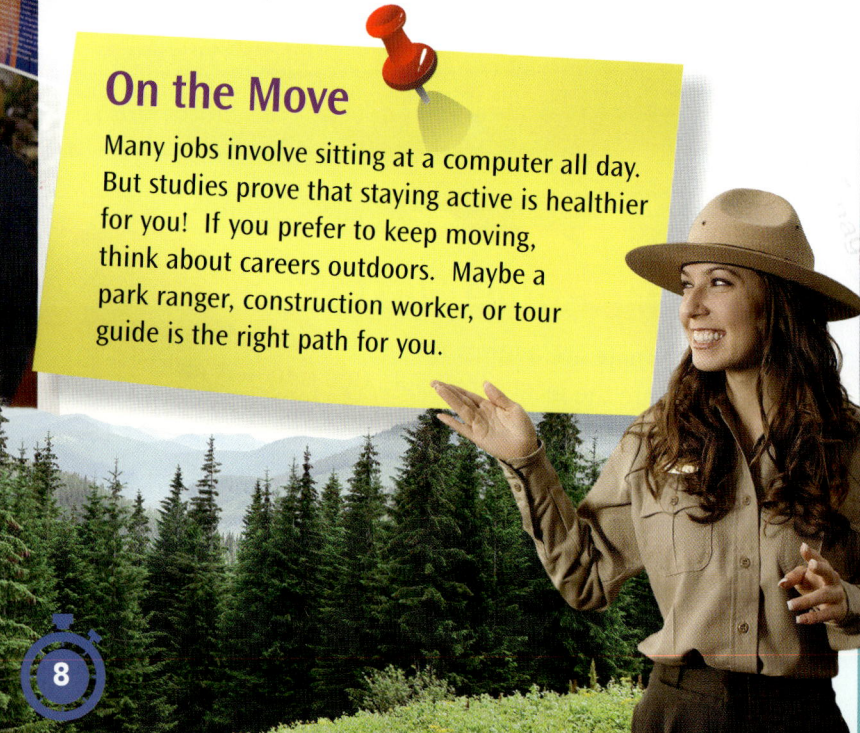

On the Move

Many jobs involve sitting at a computer all day. But studies prove that staying active is healthier for you! If you prefer to keep moving, think about careers outdoors. Maybe a park ranger, construction worker, or tour guide is the right path for you.

Happy Job

CareerBliss® helps people research and find jobs. In its recent **poll**, the people who said they were happiest at their jobs were recruiters. Recruiters help companies find new workers. Their salary is lower than average in America. These types of polls show that the person earning the most money may not be the happiest.

It is important to know what you like to do, but it is equally important to know what skills you have. Sometimes, it helps to take an **aptitude** test, but you can also find your **skill set** by just making a list.

Think about things that you do well. Some of your skills might come from the subjects you succeed at in school, but think outside of school, too. Maybe you are good with animals, or maybe you can take apart a remote control and put it back together. Perhaps you can tell when someone is upset and needs to hear a kind word. All of these skills can help you choose a career path.

Job Growth for Zoo Keepers

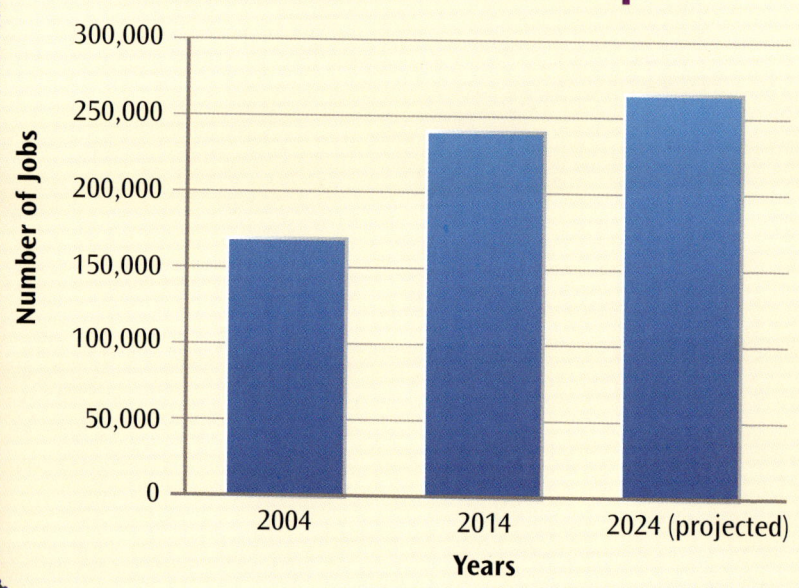

Years	Number of Jobs
2004	~170,000
2014	~237,000
2024 (projected)	~260,000

Source: Bureau of Labor and Statistics, United States Department of Labor

Zoo Crew

Veterinarians give medical care to animals. But they are not the only ones who get to spend their days with animals. In recent years, animal care workers at zoos have seen their job growth increase. This job is expected to grow faster than average over the next 10 years.

Dig Deeper: Career Aptitude Tests

Career aptitude tests ask questions that can help you figure out what career is right for you. Check out these sample questions. Think about why a career test might ask such questions.

CHOOSE THE ANSWER THAT BEST DESCRIBES YOU.

1. ☐
   - **A** I don't mind waiting for someone who is running late; everyone is late sometimes.
   - **B** It really bothers me when people are late. I don't like to have my time wasted.

2. ☐
   - **A** I will let someone know if they have hurt my feelings because it's better to be honest.
   - **B** I don't tell people if they've hurt my feelings because I don't want to make it awkward.

3. ☐
   - **A** When I have a toy that needs to be put together, I'll just start building and check the instructions if I get stuck. I'd rather learn by doing.
   - **B** When I have a toy that needs to be put together, I read all the instructions first. I like to know what I'm getting into.

4. ☐
   - **A** I do activities just to have fun with my friends and do not care if I win or lose.
   - **B** I have more fun when I win, even if it means I do not play with my friends.

5. ☐
   - **A** I find it fun and easy to talk to people I don't know.
   - **B** I find it hard and stressful to talk to people I don't know.

If most of your answers are choice "A":
You probably like to work on a team. You are driven by **intuition** and not too concerned with the rules. You value honesty and expect people to be straightforward with you.

If most of your answers are choice "B":
You probably prefer smaller groups or working alone. You value being polite and following instructions, as long as they make sense. You are thoughtful and make decisions only after careful thought.

Beliefs Matter

The best career choices line up with what we believe. Most people say that they want a career that matches their values.

In 2015, a study was done of **millennial** workers. It found that half of them would take less pay to do a job that was in line with their values. About 9 out of 10 said they wanted to use their skills to do good in the world. Many also said they would rather make less money if it meant they could work at a company that was trying to make the world a better place.

Bosses with Heart

Some people find being a leader very rewarding. CEOs are the people who have the most authority in companies. They tend to find more meaning in their jobs than other people. In a recent study, about 8 out of 10 CEOs said their jobs "make the world a better place."

Bill Gates

Rise of the Nonprofit

If you want to make the world a better place, you may want to work for a **nonprofit**. These types of organizations are all about helping others. Employment in nonprofits has been growing steadily in recent years.

Working with Purpose

Many people are happier when they are doing work that they believe in. So, another step in choosing the right career path is to determine what you value in life. Do you have a strong desire to help those less fortunate than you? Working for a nonprofit may be the right choice. Do you want to spend your days caring for children, sick people, or the elderly? Maybe working at a day care or a hospital is in your future. If you like sharing what you know with others, look into what it takes to become a teacher. Thinking through questions like these can open up a range of career choices for you.

Notable and Quotable

Daniel Burnham (shown left) was the architect behind the 1893 Chicago World's Fair. He also oversaw the building of one of the tallest skyscrapers in the nation. His advice for choosing a career path was clear. "Make no little plans; they have no magic to stir men's blood," Burnham said. "Make big plans; aim high in hope and work."

Finding Meaning

Studies show that the most fulfilling jobs involve working with others. For instance, many people say they find joy while working in health care and education. When asked, 9 out of 10 medical lab workers say their jobs have meaning.

The Right Feel

Now that you have thought about your set of values, think about the type of environment in which you want to work. Do you like focusing on one project for a long time or taking on several tasks at once? Would you rather work alone or in a group? Would you rather earn a high salary if it meant you had to work long hours? Or would you take less pay if it meant you would have more time for your family and hobbies?

Learning about your personal preferences can be helpful when thinking about which job path is right for you. As with many things in life, the first step is to learn about yourself.

Changing Your Mind

Picking the right career is an important decision. It can be hard to know what you want to do with the rest of your life. However, if you change your mind about a certain job, you will not be alone. The average American changes jobs 12 times in his or her lifetime!

Big Shifts

In 1900, 1 out of 3 members of the workforce in the United States worked on farms. By 2000, just 2 out of 10 members of the workforce worked on farms. Shifts like this are common as people's lifestyles and passions change.

The Numbers Game

By now, you probably have a good sense of what skills you have and what you like to do. The next step is to think about the practical steps to reach your goal.

Off to School

Most jobs require at least some schooling, and some require a great deal of it. Specialized health care jobs are one example. After earning **bachelor's degrees**, doctors and dentists need at least four more years of school. Then, they must train in a **clinical** setting for several years before they can work on their own. Lawyers spend an extra three years at law school after they earn their bachelor's degrees. All of this time in school is expensive. But once they are out of school, these professions tend to make more money than people in other fields.

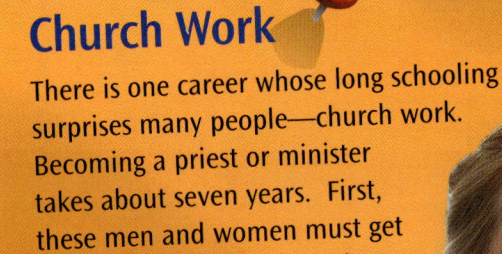

Church Work

There is one career whose long schooling surprises many people—church work. Becoming a priest or minister takes about seven years. First, these men and women must get their bachelor's degrees. Then, they go to a special school called a *seminary*.

Grad School

Six out of 10 Americans go to college. Some do not stop there. Graduate programs (often called *grad school*) teach people special skills after they have finished college. Some careers, such as professors, lawyers, and doctors, require **graduate degrees**.

College is required for many, but not all, career paths. Instead, some careers require licenses. A license is a document that says you are able to work in a certain field. You can earn a license by taking tests in certain subjects. Once you prove what you know, a group will **endorse** you for that job.

Real estate agents must have licenses to sell homes. Paramedics, hairstylists, and personal trainers also need licenses. These are great jobs if you like to work with people and would rather not spend years in school.

Work Hard

There are many ways to train for a job. But the only way to become great at one is to practice and work hard. The famed artist Michelangelo (shown left) once said, "If people knew how hard I worked to get my mastery, it wouldn't seem so wonderful after all."

Minimum Wage

In 1938, it became a federal law that all workers have to be paid above a certain amount. This amount is called a *minimum wage*. When it first began, the minimum wage was just $0.25 per hour. It did not reach $1 per hour until 1956!

Other Training

Some companies offer to train people on the job. This is especially true of careers with active **guilds** or **unions**. If you are a hands-on learner, one of these jobs may be the right choice for you.

Plumbers, electricians, and carpenters all offer on-the-job training. People often learn from others who have mastered the job. They work beside more experienced people and learn important job skills. Still, these careers take a long time to learn. Many of these careers require hundreds or even thousands of hours of training before you can work alone.

In the Union

Unions started as a way for workers to join together and fight for better pay and better working conditions. Today, fewer people are in unions. Some professions, such as teaching, still have strong unions. But many unions have closed.

Shocking

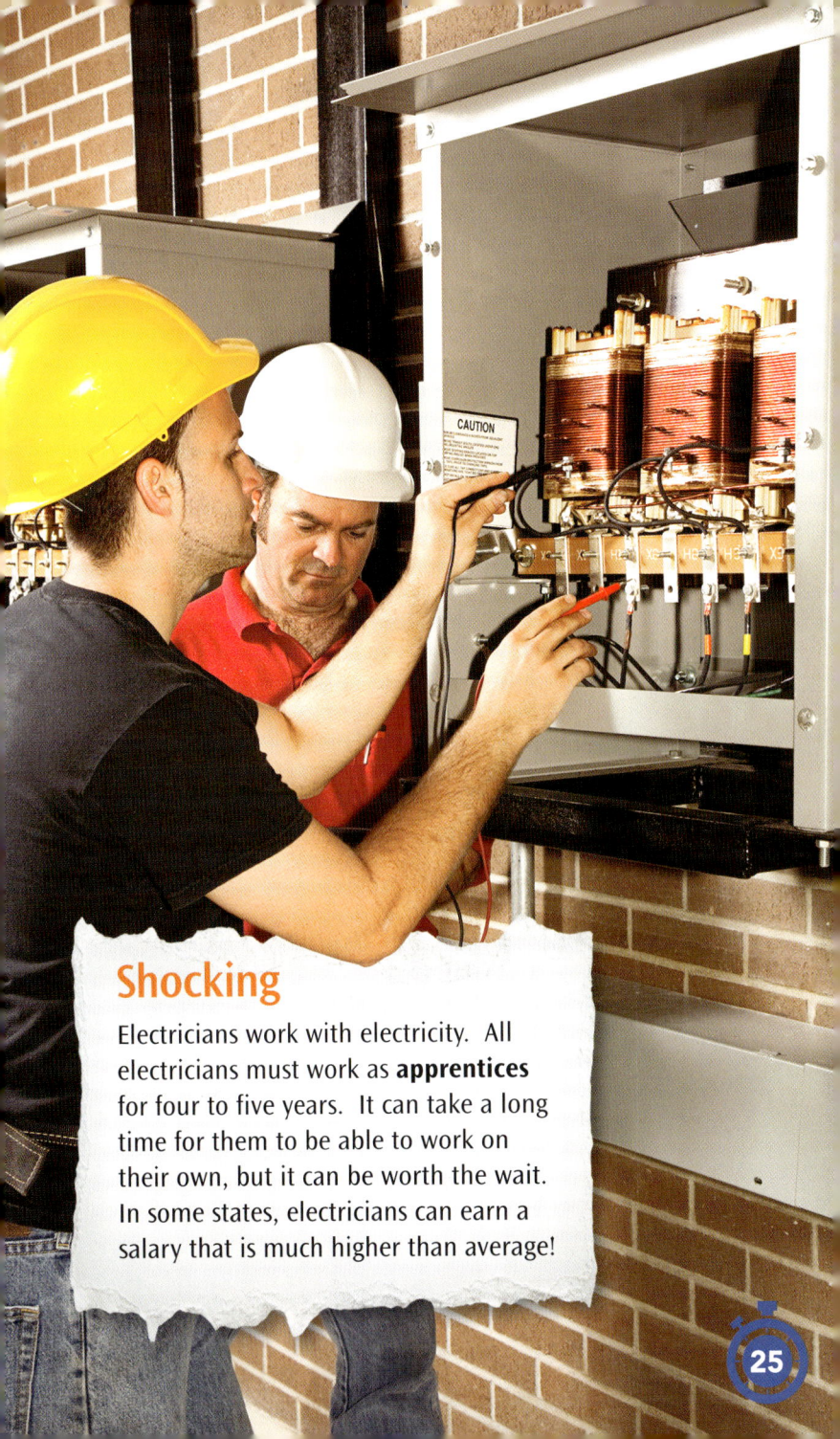

Electricians work with electricity. All electricians must work as **apprentices** for four to five years. It can take a long time for them to be able to work on their own, but it can be worth the wait. In some states, electricians can earn a salary that is much higher than average!

Show Me the Money

Pay is an important part of a career choice. You might not feel the need to get rich. But you should choose a path that will pay enough so that you can live comfortably.

Salaries vary widely in different jobs. Many high-paying jobs are in medical fields. In 2015, 9 out of 10 of the highest-paying jobs were in health care. Keep in mind that most health care jobs require many years of education. For some people, it may be worth it to pay for those years of schooling to make more money in the end. Other people may want or need to make money right out of high school. For them, jobs that require little to no additional schooling may be the best option.

Food Service

Many jobs in the food service industry (which is made up of jobs at restaurants and fast-food chains) are low paying. But even with the low pay, half of all adults in the United States will work in this field at some point in their lives. These jobs teach skills that can be applied in all career routes.

THINK LINK

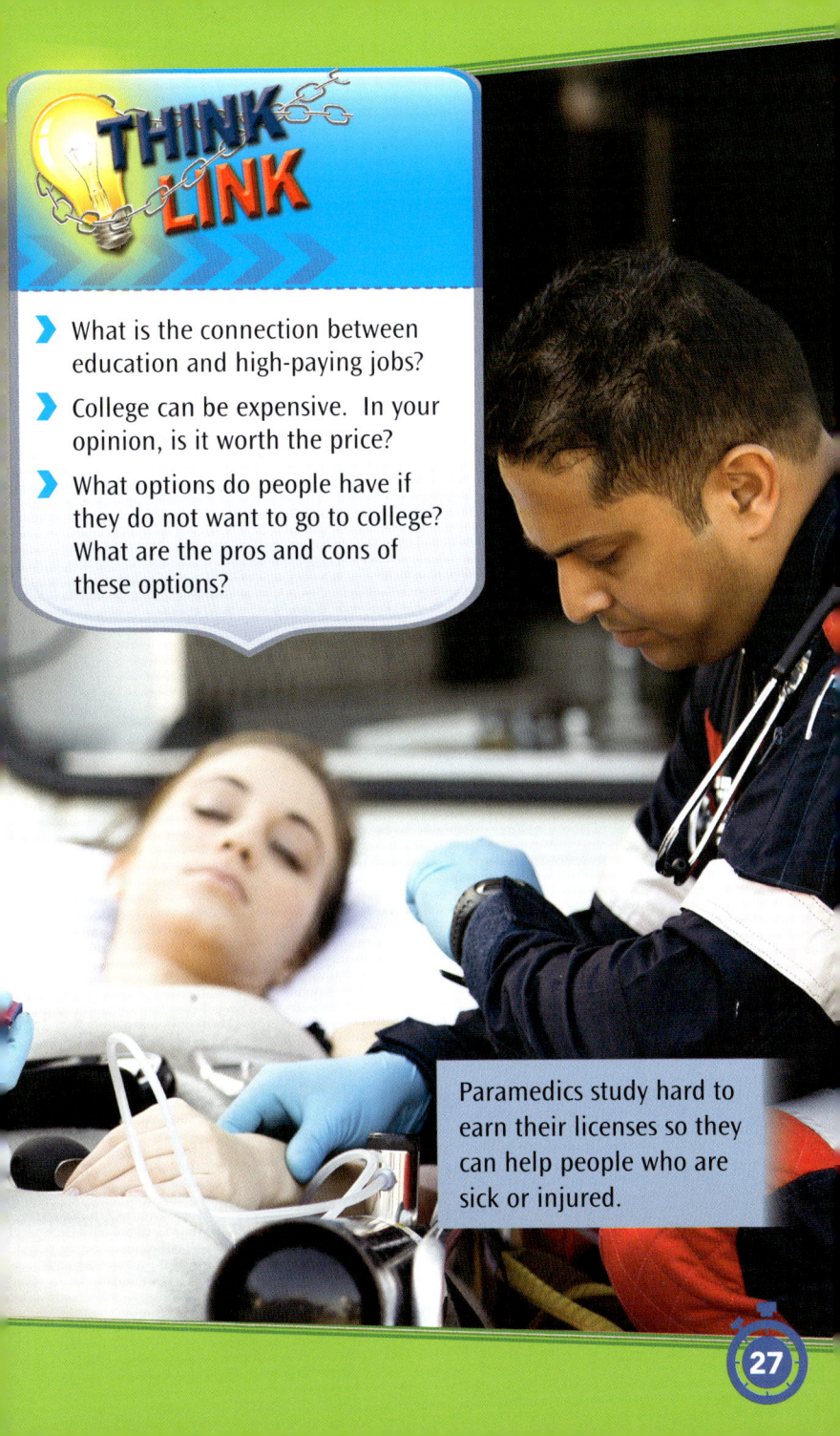

- What is the connection between education and high-paying jobs?
- College can be expensive. In your opinion, is it worth the price?
- What options do people have if they do not want to go to college? What are the pros and cons of these options?

Paramedics study hard to earn their licenses so they can help people who are sick or injured.

Job Growth

The U.S. **economy** is changing rapidly. It is important to pay attention to these changes when it becomes time to choose a career path. Some jobs are growing more than others. That means there will be more opportunities in the future.

Like high-paying jobs, many jobs with a high growth rate are in health care. Other fast-growing jobs include cartographers, or mapmakers, and financial advisors.

The best plan for your future is to take all these factors into account. Learn all you can about careers that interest you. With facts on your side, you can make a great choice.

Finding Your Way

People may not think that there is much need for maps anymore. So, it may shock them to learn that mapmaking is one of the fastest-growing jobs in the country! GPS systems rely on accurate maps to get people where they need to go. By 2024, it is expected that over 3,000 people will join this field.

STOP! THINK...

According to the U.S. government, these three jobs are projected to grow the fastest by 2024:

1. wind turbine service technicians
2. occupational therapy assistants
3. physical therapy assistants

> Wind turbine service technicians repair machines that turn wind into electricity. Why do you think it is such a fast-growing job?

> Occupational therapy assistants help people who have been sick or injured re-learn how to do daily tasks. Physical therapy assistants help people learn how to move their bodies again after injuries. What do these jobs have in common?

> Which one of these jobs sounds most interesting to you? Why?

Off the Beaten Path

Not everyone chooses a "nine-to-five" job. Today, people are paving their own, less traditional career paths. Many people want to control what kind of work they do, and when they do it.

Freedom with Freelancing

One career path is called *freelancing*. That means doing work for many companies rather than working for just one. Workers in creative fields tend to choose this route. It is popular with writers and artists. But it is also an option in science, technology, engineering, and math (STEM) fields. Some people who write computer programs choose to freelance. Many website designers do, too. It allows them to carefully choose what work they do.

Serving with Pride

One path some young people take is to join the armed forces. The United States military is made up of the Army, Navy, Marine Corps, Coast Guard, and Air Force. This path lets people serve their country while seeing the world. After two years of service, the government will pay a soldier's full tuition at a public college or university.

The Drawbacks

Freelancing is a good option for some people, but it can be hard to get started. Many people must work to save plenty of money before they decide to freelance full time. That way, if it takes them awhile to find work, they do not have to struggle.

Home Work

One career option that has become more popular in recent years is working from home. Some people may choose to work from home to avoid commuting. Others may work from home so they can care for family members.

Careers that let people work from home used to be rare. But now, many companies allow people to work outside the office. New technology has made this shift possible. About half of all U.S. workers now have the option to work from home at least some of the time. Almost 9 in 10 workers say they would like that option.

Pros and Cons of Working at Home

There are many upsides to working from home, such as saving money and time on commuting. But some people find working at home lonely. In one study, about half of freelance workers said feeling lonely made them less satisfied with their jobs.

Robot Workers?

As time goes on, more and more jobs are being automated. Some fast-food chains use computers, rather than people, to take orders. Amazon® is working to replace many of its delivery drivers with drones. Some doctors use robots to help them perform difficult surgeries.

Making Your Own Way

Another nontraditional career path is to start your own business. Startups are companies started by just one person, or a small group. Startups may seem exciting. They let people turn their dreams into great products and services.

However, starting a company, even a small one, is hard work. And it can be risky. On average, 9 out of 10 startups fail. Most people run out of money. Others find that there is not enough **demand** for their products.

Plenty of **entrepreneurs** do not let these risks get in their way. Some people start several companies before they find the right fit. In fact, studies show that a startup is more likely to succeed if its founder has at least one failed business in his or her past.

Unicorns

A startup worth $1 billion or more is known as a *unicorn*. The name comes from the fact that so few startups succeed. When one does, it is seen as magical. Famous unicorns include Spotify®, Snapchat, and Pinterest.

Started as a Startup

Many popular companies were once tiny startups. Instagram® and Facebook® both began as startups. Lyft®, which lets you hail a ride via an app, was a startup, too.

DIG DEEPER
A Roadmap to the Future

5th grade

Try new things and learn as much as possible about your interests.

8th grade

Research high school programs that interest you.

9th grade

If possible, find a summer or after-school job. Some options include mowing lawns, babysitting, or working at a local business. Take note of what you like about your job and what you do not like.

10th grade

Take classes that interest you. Research the ways in which your interests could become your career.

11th grade

Research and, if possible, visit some colleges. If college is not for you, try shadowing someone in your chosen profession for a day. Ask parents, teachers, and advisers for help.

College senior
Graduate and enter the workforce—or head back to school for more training. The sky is the limit!

College junior
Research graduate schools or jobs that may be hiring after college. Apply to graduate programs if you are interested in a career that requires one.

College sophomore
Participate! Find a college job, join clubs, and get to know your peers and teachers.

College freshman
Take some classes and see if you still want to choose that career.

12th grade
Apply to colleges, trade schools (college alternatives that teach the skills necessary for specific jobs), or talk with people working in your chosen profession.

Make a Plan

There are things you can do now to prepare for your career. That is true even if you have no clue what you want it to be yet. The most important thing is to learn as much as you can. Work hard in school, try some new hobbies, take on new challenges, and be open to inspiration. Remember that you are never locked in to one choice. You can always start over.

Many people do not find their perfect career right away. Today, J. K. Rowling is one of the most successful authors of all time. But before her Harry Potter series became a sensation, Rowling worked as a teacher and even relied on **welfare** as a single mother.

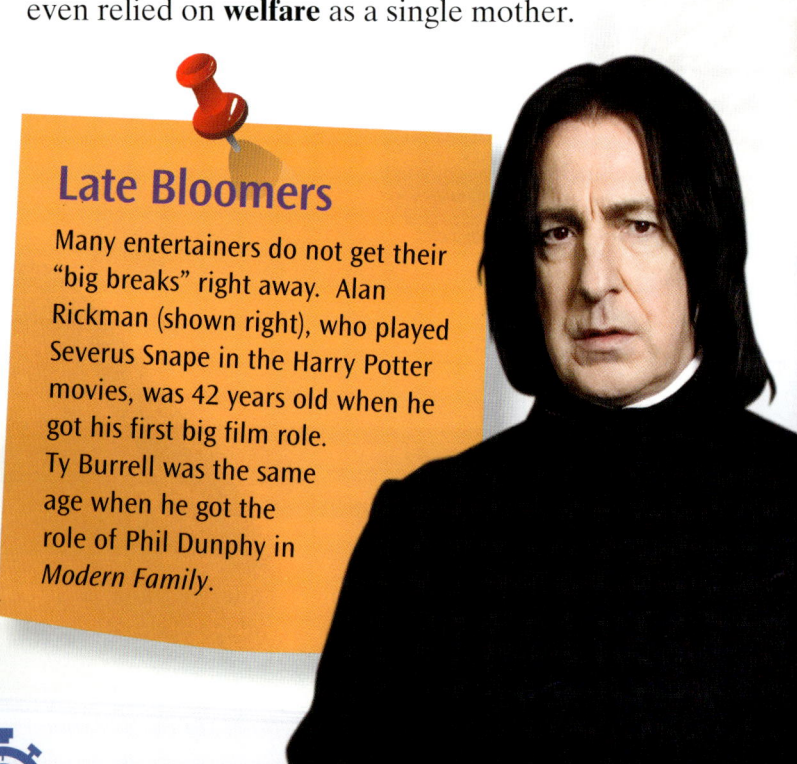

Late Bloomers

Many entertainers do not get their "big breaks" right away. Alan Rickman (shown right), who played Severus Snape in the Harry Potter movies, was 42 years old when he got his first big film role. Ty Burrell was the same age when he got the role of Phil Dunphy in *Modern Family*.

What's Your Major?

In college, your *major* is the subject that you will spend most of your time studying. When you graduate, your degree will be in that field. Most people choose their majors during the first two years of college, but about 8 in 10 students change their majors at least once.

Think again about that early morning in the future as you get ready to head to work. How do you see yourself now? Hopefully, you are excited about the day ahead. That is the best way to know you have chosen a good career. Are you looking forward to going to work? Do you feel like you are making a difference, and are you ready to take on challenges?

Facts and statistics can help you plan for the future, but the most important questions are pretty simple. What are you passionate about? What makes you feel fulfilled? Answering these two questions will take you a long way toward finding the right career.

Words of Wisdom

Franklin Roosevelt (shown left) was president of the United States during the Great Depression. That was the country's worst economic period ever. Roosevelt said that joy does not come from money. Instead, he said it comes from "the thrill of creative effort."

A Life at Work

Work is just one part of a happy life. The average person spends more than 100,000 hours working in his or her lifetime. So, it is worth finding something you love to do.

Glossary

apprentices—people who are taught a job or trade by a skilled worker

aptitude—an evaluation that is designed to show how easily someone can learn certain skills

bachelor's degrees—official documents given to students by colleges or universities usually after four years of study

clinical—relating to work done with real patients

daunting—tending to make people less confident or more afraid

demand—the need to buy goods and services

economy—the system of buying and selling goods and services

endorse—to officially or publicly say that you approve or support someone or something

entrepreneurs—people who start businesses and are willing to risk loss in order to make money

graduate degrees—official documents given to students by colleges or universities usually after one or two years of additional study following bachelor's degrees

guilds—organized groups of people who join together because they share the same jobs or interests

intuition—a natural ability that makes it possible for someone to know something without proof or evidence

millennial—term used to describe a person who was born in the 1980s or 1990s

nonprofit—organizations that do not work to make money and usually exist to help people

poll—a record taken in which many people are asked questions to find out what most people think about a subject

sectors—areas of an economy

skill set—a certain set of abilities that someone has, especially ones that can be used in a job

unions—organized groups of people that have the same purposes and interests

vague—not clear or specific in meaning

welfare—a government program that helps pay for people's food, housing, and medical costs

Index

1893 Chicago World's Fair, 16

Amazon, 33

apprentice, 25

aptitude test, 10, 12

armed forces, 30

bachelor's degrees, 20

Burnham, Daniel, 16

Burrell, Ty, 38

CareerBliss, 8–9

church, 20

college, 20–22, 26–27, 30, 36–37, 39

commute, 4

computer, 8, 30, 33

drones, 33

economy, 28

education, 17, 26–27

Einstein, Albert, 5

entrepreneurs, 34

Facebook, 35

farms, 19

finance, 6

food service, 26

freelancing, 30–31

Gates, Bill, 14

grad school, 21

graduate degrees, 21

graduate programs, 21–37

Great Depression, 40

guilds, 24

Harry Potter, 38

health, 6, 8, 17, 20, 26, 28

industries, 6–7, 26

Instagram, 35

Jobs, Steve, 5

licenses, 22

likes and dislikes, 8

Lyft, 35

major, 39

manufacturing, 6

Michelangelo, 22

millennial, 14

minimum wage, 23

Modern Family, 38

nonprofit, 15–16

Pinterest, 34

Professor Snape, 38

retail, 6

Rickman, Alan, 38

robots, 6, 33

Roosevelt, Franklin, 40

Rowling, J. K., 38

salary, 9, 18, 25

school, 8, 10, 20, 22, 26, 36–38

Snapchat, 34

Spotify, 34

startup, 34–35

STEM, 30

technology, 6, 30, 32

trade schools, 37

unicorn, 34

unions, 24

university, 30

values, 14, 18

workforce, 19, 37

work from home, 32

Check It Out!

Books

Nemelka, Blake, and Bo Nemelka. 2016. *The Middle School Student's Guide to Academic Success: 12 Conversations for College and Career Readiness.* Simon & Schuster Books for Young Readers.

Stevens, Gareth. 2008–. *Cool Careers.* Gareth Stevens Publishing.

Wigu Publishing. 2013–. *When I Grow Up I Want to Be….* Wigu Publishing.

Videos

Biz Kid$. 2008–2012. www.bizkids.com/show

Curious Kids. 2014. *Careers.* WGCU Public Media

Websites

Bureau of Labor Statistics K–12. www.bls.gov/k12

Kids.Gov Jobs & Careers. www.kids.gov/jobs

Try It!

It's Career Day, and your principal has asked you to give a presentation to the entire school! Plan a presentation that will help your fellow classmates choose their career paths.

💡 Research some key industries and find fun facts about each.

💡 Split the career options into different categories depending on what students will need to do, such as: become an apprentice, earn a bachelor's degree, earn a graduate degree, earn a license, or graduate from a trade school.

💡 Create a fun and engaging slideshow presentation with at least five different career options and paths.

About the Author

Heather Price-Wright is a writer and editor living in New York City. She has known she wanted to write for a living since she was in the first grade, and has worked toward that goal ever since. She has a degree in English and creative writing. Price-Wright has held lots of jobs, including the 4 a.m. shift in a bagel shop, before her writing career. Now, she writes about history, current events, science, and politics for young readers.